D1012975

WAIT FOR ME

and other poems about
the irritations and consolations
of a long marriage

JUDITH VIORST

ILLUSTRATIONS BY STEPHEN CAMPBELL

SIMON & SCHUSTER
NEW YORK   LONDON   TORONTO   SYDNEY   NEW DELHI

Simon & Schuster
1230 Avenue of the Americas
New York, NY 10020

Copyright © 2015 by Judith Viorst

All rights reserved, including the right to reproduce this book or portions thereof
in any form whatsoever. For information, address Simon & Schuster Subsidiary
Rights Department, 1230 Avenue of the Americas, New York, NY 10020

First Simon & Schuster hardcover edition October 2015

SIMON & SCHUSTER and colophon are registered trademarks of Simon & Schuster, Inc.

For information about special discounts for bulk purchases,
please contact Simon & Schuster Special Sales at
1-866-506-1949 or business@simonandschuster.com.

The Simon & Schuster Speakers Bureau can bring authors
to your live event. For more information or to book an event,
contact the Simon & Schuster Speakers Bureau at
1-866-248-3049 or visit our website at www.simonspeakers.com.

Interior design by Ruth Lee-Mui

Manufactured in the United States of America

1   3   5   7   9   10   8   6   4   2

Library of Congress Cataloging-in-Publication Data

Viorst, Judith.
Wait for me : and other poems about the irritations and
consolations of a long marriage / Judith Viorst.
  pages ; cm
  I. Title.
  PS3572.I6   A6   2015
  811'.54   2015009838

ISBN 978-1-4767-9308-5
ISBN 978-1-4767-9309-2 (ebook)

This book is dedicated to the memory of these long marriages:

Hanna and Peter Altman

Ann and Howard Bray

Ruth and Mortimer Caplin

Natalie and Sey Chassler

Betsy and Alan Cohn

Jackie and Larry Dunkel

Phyllis and Henry Hersh

Ellie and Norman Horwitz

Silvia and Marvin Koner

Judy and Allen Mossman

Lee and Larry Ramer

Barbara and Steve Rosenfeld

Lisbeth and Daniel Schorr

CONTENTS

THE
IRRITATIONS

It destroys one's nerves to be amiable

every day to the same human being.

—Benjamin Disraeli

FINISHED?

Just make sure she finishes your thoughts and you finish hers. That's all you need.

—Elizabeth Kostova

In our first years we completed each other's sentences
And took delight in being so deeply known.
But now we're often saying, in a most undelighted tone,
Could you please stop interrupting, and let me finish.

And when I am making a point at some dinner party,
Directing it to the man on my left, not to you,
Where do you get the gall to jump right in before I am through?
You have to let me finish, and stop interrupting!

And when you're about to mess up the joke that you're telling
And all I'm trying to do is help you out
By amplifying, clarifying—there is no need to shout
That I should let you finish, and stop interrupting!

Decades of cohabitation have failed to diminish
This clash between interrupter and interruptee,
For whenever we try to discuss it, I interrupt you and
    you interrupt me,
And we never agree to let each other finish.

THE OTHER GUY

**How can a woman be expected to be happy with a man who insists
on treating her as if she were a perfectly rational being?**

—Oscar Wilde

I guess it's too late to tell you that I've changed my
    mind, that I should have married the other guy,
The one who worshipped the ground on which I walked,
The one who listened, enraptured, when I talked, and agreed
    with everything I was saying.

How blissful life would have been if I had only had the
    good sense to marry the other guy,
The one who saw nothing about me to criticize,
Who found perfection in everything from the circumference
    of my thighs to my salad dressing.

How smoothly things would have gone if, when he proposed,
    I'd chosen to be the wife of the other guy,
The one with whom I could mentally relax,
The one who wouldn't be challenging my facts or correcting
    the way I pronounce "hegemony."

How come I didn't know, fifty years ago, that I shouldn't
    be saying no to the other guy?
How I'd have loved being mindlessly adored!
And yet I keep suspecting I'd have been bored, bored,
    bored, bored, bored out of my mind.

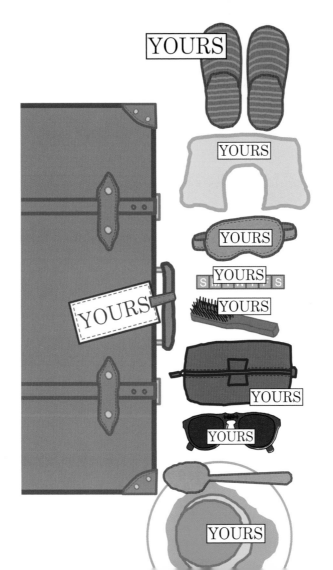

LINES COMPOSED WHILE PACKING TO GO ON VACATION

Let there be spaces in your togetherness. . . .
Fill each other's cup but drink not from one cup.

—Kahlil Gibran

Although I'm exceedingly fair,
I simply do not like to share
A closet, a dresser drawer, or a bathroom shelf.
But any time you'd like to count,
You'll find the exact same amount
Of space that is yours and the space that I've kept
    for myself.

It's a matter of personal pride
That whenever I'm asked to divide
A vegetable curry or a sashimi matsu,
I will carefully calculate
The portion I put on each plate
So there isn't a drop more for me than there is for you.

Yet in spite of all this you still scowl
When I don't want you using my towel
Or won't go along with two spoons and one crème
    caramel.
There's a you and a me and an us
And the reason for all of this fuss
Is I have firm boundaries and yours are as porous
    as hell.

In a marriage there's sharing enough
Without intermingling stuff
Like hairbrushes, house keys, the spray that you
    spray up your nose.
And equal but separate works fine
As a way to keep what is mine mine.
So don't even ask if my suitcase has room for your clothes.

ONLY TRYING TO HELP

The truth will set you free, but first it will piss you off.

—Gloria Steinem

I'm only trying to help
When I observe that every tie that you wear has been stained
By food you have failed to transport to your mouth from your plate.
And you're only trying to help when you tell me I've gained,
Along with a lifetime of wisdom, a bit too much weight.
And when I complain that I'm tired of having to shriek
Because you insist that a hearing aid won't help you hear,
Please know I mean well with each chastising word that I speak
Into your left (and your only viable) ear.
And when you remind me of things I forgot to get done,
Like turning the eggs off and paying the telephone bill,
And when I inform you of how many stop signs you've run,
Let's try to remember our hearts are suffused with goodwill.
With always the best of intentions we've never refrained
From our earnest attempts to constantly upgrade our mate.
And though there are times when our marital bonds have been
    strained
By our unerring talent to mutually irritate,
We find comfort in knowing we're only trying to help.

AGAIN

The essential matrimonial facts: that to be happy you have to find variety in repetition.

—Jeffrey Eugenides

asked

You're telling that story again?
You're actually telling that story again?
You keep on slipping it into conversations.
Though they haven't heard it before,
I've heard it before. And before. And before.
And before—there must be a statute of limitations
On how many times a person
Expects the person that person's been married to
Forever, or at least since way back when,
To listen to a story,
The same old story,
The same damn story,
Over and over
And over and over
Again.

answered

I'm telling that story again!
That's right—I'm telling that story again.
It livens up a lot of conversations.
And they haven't heard it before.
Too bad for you if you've heard it before.
Guess what? There *is* no statute of limitations
On how many times a person
And the person that person's been married to
Forever, or at least since way back when,
Must listen to each other's stories,
Those same old stories,
Those same damn stories,
Over and over
And over and over

And over

And over

And over

And over

And over

And over

And over

And over

And over

And over

And over

And over

And over

And over

And over

And over

Again.

AND A FEW MORE ISSUES

Marriage is an alliance entered into by a man who can't sleep with the window shut, and a woman who can't sleep with the window open.

—George Bernard Shaw

I say it's too cold in the bedroom.
You say it's too hot.
I beg you to give that old jacket away.
You will not.
And why are we walking eight blocks?
Through the rain? In the dark?
Because you've ignored my entreaties
To please valet park.
Through decades and decades of failing
To see eye to eye,
Our marriage keeps on keeping on
And I'm wondering why.

You're proud of your honest opinions.
I'd say that they lacked
That social veneer I keep trying to teach you,
Called tact.
And though I regard being ten minutes late
As a crime,
You're claiming that ten minutes late is the same
As on time.
So how can it possibly be
That we've lasted this long
When it is so hard to agree on who's right,
And who's wrong?

You're sulking because I have dragged you
To Wagner again.
I'm sulking because you are making me
Watch Yale play Penn.
Our tastes, styles, and judgments
On many occasions diverge.
But when I consider departing,
I stifle the urge,
Refusing to give up the hope that
There will come a day
I'll finally persuade you to see things
Exactly my way.

THE
CONSOLATIONS

In every marriage more than a week old, there
are grounds for divorce. The trick is to find,
and continue to find, grounds for marriage.

—Robert Anderson

NICE

**One cannot spend one's time in being modern when there
are so many more important things to be.**

—Wallace Stevens

In a world where there are children named Buster and
    Apple,
And nobody knows any Yettas anymore,
It's nice to be married to someone the same age
    as I am.

In a world where, whenever there's talk about folks
    who are famous,
And I haven't a clue as to what they're famous for,
It's nice to be married to someone as clueless
    as I am.

In a world where regular people have personal trainers,
And it takes a size zero to make a woman feel thin,
It's nice that you are expanding as quickly as I am.

In a world where bottled water is an accessory,
And plain old club soda preferred over something
    with gin,
It's nice you're as unabstemious as I am.

In a world where everyone's vegan or vegetarian,
Or else has a list a mile long of what they don't eat,
It's nice that you're as omnivorous as I am.

In a world where virtual is the new reality,
And telephone booths are virtually obsolete,
It's nice that you're every bit as unwired as I am.

In a world where everyone's powering on and off,
In a world where hacking doesn't refer to a cough,
In a world where nothing on earth is too arcane
For Google to instantaneously explain,
And tattoos aren't only for thugs but for the elite,
It's nice you're as twentieth-century,
As stubbornly twentieth-century,
As hopelessly twentieth-century as I am.

ACCUSTOMED

You often felt the unbearable need for another body . . . to drop his things around the room in a way that was maddening but still served as a reminder that he was there.

—Meg Wolitzer

In addition to your face,
I've grown accustomed to the cacophony of your snore.
And your bony knees pressing into the small of my back.
And your toenail clippings adorning our tiled bathroom
    floor.
And those crumbs in the kitchen revealing you just snuck
    a snack.
And me tripping over your always un-put-away shoes.
And your desk: A nightmare! A criminal act! A disgrace!
And your voice too loudly expressing contrarian views.
And your face—your baggy-eyed, beloved face.

THE WIDOW

You had to work hard to prevent your mind from sabotaging you by its looking hungrily back at the superabundant past.

—Philip Roth

The widow moves from her house with its too many
    stairs and its excess of rooms to a modern apartment,
Divesting herself of a lifetime of treasures and trash.
Takes classes in Spanish, cosmology, and Jane Austen.
Reminds herself, whenever she's going somewhere,
That she's now the one in charge of making sure that she
    has the keys and also some cash. And that she knows
How to get where she's going.

The widow buys season tickets to the symphony, to the
    theater, to the opera,
And signs up for cruises, seeking a like-minded friend
To join her, to be her companion, so very careful not to
    depend upon
Her devoted but so-very-busy sons and daughters.

The widow takes pains to conceal the less appealing of her
      fears and faults and foibles.
Who but a long-married husband puts up with that stuff?
Who but a long-married husband could have loved her
      enough, understood her enough,
To believe—at least some of the time—that she was worth it?

The widow keeps up with the news and holds strong views,
      but there's no one to argue with at breakfast,
Nor is she looking for someone on Dating.com.
And if she should hint that she might be in the market,
She's greeted with "You must be kidding, Mom," and an
      invitation to visit the grandchildren.

The widow masters the art of sleeping alone and waking alone.
Masters the art of going to movies alone.
Masters the art of a glass of wine, a place mat, and a
    cloth napkin even when she's eating dinner alone.
Considers getting a cat so she won't be alone.
Wonders who, if she needed someone to drive her to the
    ER, she would ask to drive.
And reminds me once again how lucky I am, how happy
    I am, how incredibly grateful I am
That you are alive.

OTHER BEDS

There is almost no marital problem that can't be helped enormously by taking off your clothes.

—Garrison Keillor

So maybe practice makes perfect.
Maybe custom does not stale.
Maybe familiarity breeds no contempt.
Maybe they never get tired.
Maybe their bodies never fail
To achieve whatever it is that they attempt.

Maybe they aren't required
To acquire prescription meds
For the pepping up of their less-than-peppy powers.
And maybe we shouldn't wonder
What's going on in other beds
When we could be getting something going in ours.

LIKE TWO SHIPS THAT PASS IN THE NIGHT

Two are better than one. . . . If either of them falls down, one can help the other up. Also, if two lie down together, they will keep warm. But how can one keep warm alone?

—Ecclesiastes 4:9–11

Like two ships that pass in the night,
We pass each other on our way to the bathroom,
Never pausing to say hello or to kiss.
It is three, it is four, it is five o'clock in the morning,
And how we wish that we could stop meeting like this,
Exhausted, shuffling, and barely able to see,
Driven from bed by the urgent need to pee.

We are not at our boudoir-best.
You wear plaid pajamas, while I sleep in T-shirts
That say things like GLOBAL WARMING—IT'S THE TRUTH!
But no silks or satins or laces could help us recover
The undisturbed slumbers of our long-vanished youth.
Too tired to linger and too tired to rush,
We do what we came to do, and remember to flush.

Awake yet again, we get up
To head—yet again—to the same destination.
I maybe nod, and you maybe wave a hand.
When we turned off the lights and lay down our heads on our
    pillows,
These nocturnal rendezvous were not what we'd planned.
Yet the sight of each other is a most comforting sight.
Like those ships, we're glad we're not alone in the night.

WAIT
FOR ME

She "made it very clear to him that she would see
him again in Heaven someday. . . . But he was
worried about how he would find her. So they made
a plan to meet in the front left corner of Heaven."

—Jerome Groopman, "Lives Less Ordinary," *The New Yorker*

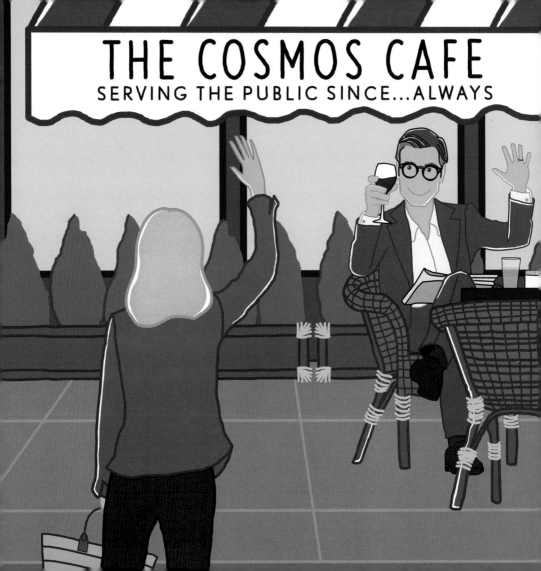

So just in case there's a place where we go when we die,

And just in case you should get there before I do,

I don't, when it's my turn, want to spend eternity

looking for you.

So let's decide where we'll meet. Let's decide

Where you'll wait for me.

You know I have a terrible sense of direction
And get confused whenever I go someplace new,
Which means I could be wandering through infinity
searching for you.

So let's choose a simple location
Where you will wait for me.

This isn't to say that our final days are impending.
I'm simply trying to cross a few things off my list.
And one of those things is our inescapable ending,
Which, each time I bring up the subject, you always resist.
So no, I'm not going all dark and gloomy and Russian.
I just, as you know, don't like leaving matters to chance.
And that's why I want to embark on a brief discussion
Of where we'll be dancing after our closing dance.

For I'm told till death do us part is just for sissies
And true lovers stay together long after that.
But how can we stay together if I don't even know where
you're at?

Sit down, and let's figure out
Where you're going to wait for me.

I'm on to all of your tricks of procrastination,

So don't expect to avoid this pre-mortem chat.

And don't you start reading the paper when I'm trying

to have a chat.

Could you put it down? Now! Let's decide

Where you will wait for me.

Your thoughts about bank regulation are quite persuasive,

And so are your points about climate change and world peace.

But I'm finding your comments exceedingly evasive

When I want to discuss what happens when both of us cease.

I'm trying to figure out how we're getting together

Across the bewildering vastness of time and space,

While you've just turned on the TV to check on the weather,

With that give-me-a-break expression on your face.

Yes, okay, I do understand your irritation
At my compulsive need to be planning ahead.
But could you kindly stop telling me to live in
the moment instead?

I don't need a moment—I need a place
Where you'll wait for me.

And another reason you hate this conversation
Is because you think all those treadmill miles you tread
Will save you, along with your morning oat bran, from
ever being dead.

Well, they won't. And you will. Pick a place
Where you will wait for me.

How has this marriage endured? It is more than surprising.

You are a last-minute person while I am a first.

I need a schedule. You much prefer improvising,

And hope without fail for the best, while I gird for the
worst.

I guess we've counted a lot on attraction and laughter

And the mess and marvel of family entanglement.

But—damn it!—we should be talking about what comes after,

Which troubles me much more than what already went.

I've accepted that we've grown old, not merely older,

And that we depend on ten different pills to thrive,

And that our once-perky body parts have long ago taken

a dive.

I am fine with all that. I just must know

Where you'll wait for me.

FOR
SALE

FOR SALE
555-3420

I've accepted that our children act like our parents,

And that, when they get together, they will contrive

New arguments to persuade us that we should sell our house

and not drive.

I don't want to hear it. I want to hear

Where you'll wait for me.

We still enjoy holding hands when we're watching a movie.

We still enjoy holding hands when we walk down a street.

And though it's been decades since we've aspired to groovy,

We're not quite prepared yet for "Look at them! Aren't they

sweet!"

But what with the acid reflux and spinal stenosis

And completely forgetting last evening's dinner date,

Don't tell me that I am suffering from a neurosis

If I say we're in a somewhat diminished state.

Last week you misplaced the car in underground parking.

With one fatal click, I wiped a file from my screen.

We need to accept reality: our brains are no longer that

keen.

So while we still can, let's decide on

Where you will wait for me.

The time wasted searching for house keys is pathetic!
The time wasted searching for eyeglasses? Obscene!
But I find these lessons instructive because I'm taking
them to mean

We should pick out—and write down!—exactly
Where you'll wait for me.

We've put in a grab bar to grab while we're taking showers,

And a railing to keep us from falling down the stairs.

We're more inclined to deplore this decline of our powers

Than be grateful for early-bird specials and senior fares.

But we shouldn't bother dwelling on time's depredations

Because, as that dumb saying goes, it is what it is.

And maybe an afterwards will provide reparations

For whatever the present moments lack in fizz.

HEAVENLY
BALLOON
TOURS

And maybe a person could spend forever proving

That happily ever after isn't a myth.

But since you're the one I want to be happily ever

after with,

Give in. Just give in. And let's choose a place

Where you'll wait for me.

Or am I presuming too much when I presume that
I am your number one choice, not second, not fifth,
On your list of those you most prefer to be everlastingly
with.

Am I right? Say I'm right! Then figure out
Where you'll wait for me.

We've been through "I told you it wasn't worth all that money."

We've been through "For once in your life admit that you're wrong!"

We've been through "You actually thought that movie was funny?"

But more often than not, we find that we sing the same song.

And most of the time, what's good overrides aggravation,

And so far we've somehow escaped some really close calls,

Suggesting we're in this together for a duration

That could continue long after the curtain falls.

Do we believe in Heaven? I don't think so.

In fact, we probably don't. And yet. And yet.

How could it possibly hurt to hedge this bet?

Come closer, my darling, and we'll decide

Where you'll wait for me.

ABOUT THE AUTHOR

JUDITH VIORST was born and brought up in New Jersey, graduated from Rutgers University, moved to Greenwich Village, and has lived in Washington, D.C., since 1960, when she married Milton Viorst, a political writer. They have three sons and seven grandchildren. A 1981 graduate of the Washington Psychoanalytic Institute, Viorst writes in many different areas: science books; children's picture books—including the beloved *Alexander and the Terrible, Horrible, No Good, Very Bad Day*; adult fiction and nonfiction; poetry for children and adults; and musical theater.

ALSO BY JUDITH VIORST

Poems

The Village Square

It's Hard to Be Hip Over Thirty and Other Tragedies of Married Life

People and Other Aggravations

How Did I Get to Be Forty and Other Atrocities

If I Were in Charge of the World and Other Worries

When Did I Stop Being Twenty and Other Injustices

Forever Fifty and Other Negotiations

Sad Underwear and Other Complications

Suddenly Sixty and Other Shocks of Later Life

I'm Too Young to Be Seventy and Other Delusions

Unexpectedly Eighty and Other Adaptations

Children's Books

Sunday Morning

I'll Fix Anthony

Try It Again, Sam

The Tenth Good Thing About Barney

Alexander and the Terrible, Horrible, No Good, Very Bad Day

My Mama Says There Aren't Any Zombies, Ghosts, Vampires, Creatures, Demons, Monsters, Fiends, Goblins, or Things

Rosie and Michael

Alexander, Who Used to Be Rich Last Sunday

The Good-bye Book

Earrings!

The Alphabet from Z to A (With Much Confusion on the Way)

Other

Yes, Married

A Visit from St. Nicholas (To a Liberated Household)

Love & Guilt & the Meaning of Life, Etc.

Necessary Losses

Murdering Mr. Monti

Imperfect Control

You're Officially a Grown-Up

Grown-Up Marriage

Alexander and the Wonderful, Marvelous, Excellent, Terrific Ninety Days